Praise for *The R*

"Scrap gardens, metal shards, blankets of r___ ___ity collapsing, a house shut against itself, everywhere fragile bodies. A chronic cough, corrosion, exhaustion haunting the landscape. In a story too painful to tell, in a flood of stories so small yet so heavy that only archetypes can carry their weight (The Oldest Sister, The Quiet Mother), in increments of time so grand, so trivial (The Century of Silences, Spring Cleaning), Rochelle Hurt manifests shifts of perspective that are at once tectonic and barely perceptible. Her portrait of the hapless Rusted City and its inhabitants is unsettling, provocative, visionary, its magic hard won—a phoenix rising out of ash."

—Holly Iglesias

"In Hurt's sparkling debut, the tinny, melancholic, gorgeous stir of Baudelaire's heartbroken metropolis is heard again, but this time its flesh and spirit are rusted. Its lung is rusted, its heart and belly are rusted. Its mother, father, and sister are all rusted. In this city, though, rust is no death rattle but the life rustle. In this city, the prose poem scrapes the sky until rusted clouds burst, sending rusted beauty clattering down. Hurt brings the prose poem back to life."

—Sabrina Orah Mark

"Through the tiny window of the prose poem, *The Rusted City* paints a surreal landscape of an alternate Midwestern Rust Belt. Small domestic events resonate with the description of centuries (eons even) of the city's history, causing macro and micro levels of sense-making in this strange, beautiful, and heart-breaking world. Through surprising image and impeccable timing, Rochelle Hurt has somehow managed to make a single family into an apt metaphor for American life. *The Rusted City* is outstanding, unique, and new—one of the best books I've read this year.

—Sarah Messer

The Rusted City

The
Rusted City

a novel in poems

Rochelle Hurt

WHITE PINE PRESS / BUFFALO, NEW YORK

White Pine Press
P.O. Box 236
Buffalo, New York 14201
www.whitepine.org

Grateful acknowledgement is made to the following journals, in which these
poems first appeared:
The Cincinnati Review: "The Favorite Father Gets Home from Work," "The Quiet
Mother Cups the Favorite Father's Ear," "The Smallest Sister Decides to Make
Herself Red," "The Quiet Mother Hides." *Inch:* "In the Century of Mute
Tongues" and "In the Century of New Skin." *Mid-American Review:* "In the Century
of Fumes." *New Delta Review:* "The Smallest Sister Plays" under the title "Infection:
My Sister Plays." *Superstition Review:* "In the Century of Birthmarks," "In the
Century of Lunch Pails," "In the Century of Mandatory Crying," "In the Century
of Rust." *The Portland Review:* "The Oldest Sister is an Indian Giver." *The Prose Poem
Project:* "The Smallest Sister Meets the Favorite Father," "The Oldest Sister
Smashes Cans," "At the Edge of the City." *Versal:* "The Old Mill."

Publication of this book was made possible by support from Robert
Alexander and with public funds from the New York State Council on
the Arts, a State Agency.

Cover art: *Throne.* Copyright ©2014 by Sharon Pazner
Cover design: Jennika Smith
Editorial Intern: Christine Woodell

First Edition.

ISBN: 978-1-935210-52-8

Printed and bound in the United States of America.

Library of Congress Control Number: 2013942904

Marie Alexander Series, Volume 18
    Robert Alexander, Series Editor
    Nickole Brown, Editor

I am grateful for support from my family, especially my mother, who has made all things possible for me. Special thanks also go to Doug Diesenhaus for his continued support of my work.

Sarah Messer deserves special mention for her creative guidance on this project, as well as Malena Mörling for her advice and support.

I am also grateful to Mark Cox, Michael White, Lavonne Adams, and all of the faculty, students, and staff in the Creative Writing Department at UNC Wilmington.

Thank you to Nickole Brown and Robert Alexander for their belief in this book, and to the Marie Alexander Series and White Pine Press for making it happen. I am especially grateful to Nickole for her editorial guidance.

I am also grateful to the Jentel Artist Residency Program for their generous support.

Thank you to Matt Bell and Dzanc Books/The Collagist for their kindness.

Thanks also go to Sharon Pazner for lending her beautiful art to the book.

for Youngstown, City of Homes

Contents

I

II

III

IV

V

The Old Mill

is where the birds live, the smallest sister tells her mother. "I saw them weaving baskets in the eaves." The quiet mother slides a thread between her lips and sucks a minute, as if on licorice. She's working on a slipcover. "That's impossible—" she says, eyes crossed on the thread she now pulls from her mouth, "they're gone."

The smallest sister shakes her head, a spring-hinged door swinging as the birds flit in and out and in. On the floorboards, a shadow show unfolds while the quiet mother weaves a needle into her hand, and mends. The shrubs peck quietly at the window. Steel mill, still mill, sill mill, the smallest sister thinks. The birds are there, eating the rust from their wings.

The Quiet Mother Smiles

as she tells her two daughters of the favorite father. "He'll be your favorite, too," she says, smoothing her hair with her palm. The smallest watches as red dust brushed loose falls from her mother's head and collects on the kitchen tile, already stained a dull orange.

"You'd better clean your ring," the oldest mumbles, sweeping her hand along the wall on her way out of the room. One half of the ceiling caves in after her, but the quiet mother still smiles. She smiles until her tired teeth sink into her gums. "This one will work," she says. Sun pours through the hole in the ceiling like bleach over the room, washing the tile back to white for a moment.

The quiet mother tugs a gold ring from one of her fingers and hands it to the smallest sister. The ring is heavy as a marble in the smallest sister's hand, and heavier every minute—a rock, anxious to be let go. The quiet mother picks chips of rust from where the ring had hugged her finger and blows on it like something too hot, sending a storm of red to the floor.

The Smallest Sister Goes to School

with a stone in her hand. Fool's gold. She thinks of it as a light bulb because when she cradles it, her palms glow a pale yellow. She tries to show this to the other girls in the darkened coat closet. She parts her clasped thumbs and peeks into the bottomless night of her hands, but the rock is broken—now just a chunk of painted coal. The others don't understand. The smallest sister climbs into her handmade dark then and pulls her fingers tight around her.

The City Swallows

falling scraps like a dog at a dinner table, its river tongue-lapping them in from the lip of the shore. It jostles them down its throat, shaking an old tune out as the scraps rub and clash their way underground, groaning into their beds of dirt. This is the din that's rattled centuries of the city's floorboards. But as far as the smallest sister knows, it is only the cymbal hymn the earth has always been humming—the same thrum the doubtful doctors heard from her mouth the day she was born. A hundred ears to her infant chest, and the whole town confirmed: the sound of the city throbbed inside her.

Outside, the Smallest Sister Hugs

the factory walls. She watches through a window as crane arms dip
and curl over an ocean of fathers lining up to be caught like so many
babies to be born. Wearing their hard hats like cauls, they bob and
jimmy and john their way into the world outside through a chute.
Birthed backwards, they come out tarnished and life licks them new
again—new enough for daughters to touch. The smallest sister
counts as they spill into the parking lot, waiting to be claimed.
One-one-thousand, two-one-thousand, three-one-thousand fathers
on the ground. The orange tips of their cigarettes float and flick
around their bodies like fire moths. Bright as a heads-up penny,
she spots the one she wants in a heap of coughs, his skin already
baby-red with rust.

The Oldest Sister Smashes Cans

on the sidewalk with her spindly boyfriend. They crunch them beneath their feet, dancing to the clatter of aluminum crumpling. Each can lets out a wheeze as it folds into itself, a burst of breath that whooshes the rust-laced pollen on the ground around it away, clearing a spot of pavement. Soon a long stretch of sidewalk is dotted with flattened cans, glinting silver among the red.

The smallest sister has been watching, counting the cans dead. She spots one yet half-crushed. "Here," she says to the oldest sister, and points to the can at her feet. "This one's still living."

"You do it," the oldest sister says.

So the smallest sister lifts her left foot, sees the metal shell turn dull in her shadow, and steps on it, quick. The top tab snaps off and laughter flings into the air with a ping. The smallest sister picks the tab up and shoves it in her pocket like a dime, as the oldest sister's boyfriend unravels with laughter, draping the scene: laughter cast across the sidewalk, laughter lying in strings, laughter strewn like garlands over crowds of crushed aluminum.

The Smallest Sister Meets the Favorite Father

and he is perfect. He is all clanging and steam. He is in the kitchen, sorting through pipes beneath the sink. She follows him out to the heat-wilted yard, where he solders his feet to the soil with guilt. "I'm going to stay this time," he says to himself, not sure yet how to speak the language of daughters. The smallest sister reaches down and wipes the red dust from his work boot. She studies the way it settles into the grooves on her fingertip. It looks like a solar system, a red-ringed universe—or a wound, glowing orange, seething. "My favorite," she says.

The Quiet Mother Cups the Favorite Father's Ear

with her lip. It quivers on her tongue like a lump of pudding, a tapioca earlobe. The smallest sister is behind the wall, watching through a termite hole. She sees their hands and legs tangle into a knot of twine binding itself to the bed. When one of the hands reaches up and ties itself to the chain in the ceiling, black spills into the room. The smallest sister gasps, and shreds of rust flutter from the peephole into her mouth. They snag their way down, crumpling like foil in her throat.

Wife Song

Once you were silver,
skin-tease and flash.

I could reach inside
your chest, empty

as a tin canister, the air
thick with echo. I could stretch

my fingers out and tap
my nail against your heart,

which hung like a spoon
from your ribcage.

Once I tapped too hard,
and it clattered to the bottom

of your gut. I spent months
trying to hang it back up.

The Smallest Sister Spots an Iris

she must have. This one is still blue, a new late bloom, not yet clothed in red. Every flower in the scrap garden is red—bluebells, lilacs, daffodils, violets—except this iris.

She reaches for it, sliding her arm between two sword-leaves, and grasps its stem, stiff in her hand. She pulls until the stem begins to split like a cable, shedding wiry fibers. Stubborn in its roots, the iris doesn't give. So she digs a sliver of pig iron from the soil, tiny but sharp enough. Holding the frayed stem in one hand, she presses the iron shard against it and cuts the iris loose.

Red dust has already begun to collect in its center like an idea. A bright red heart has formed on the head of the yellow pistil, pumping her through with dread.

The Only Solution

is to trick him into touching her. At home in her room, iris in hand, the smallest sister licks her finger, dips it in the bowl of red at the flower's center, and smears its rusty pollen in a line across her palm.

In the kitchen, the favorite father is a wall of heavy breath and denim before her. "My hand," she says, clutching it to her stomach. "I cut it in the scrap garden."

The favorite father bends at his knees, crouching down to see inside his daughter's hand, squeezed into a pink fist. "I can't open it," she says, so he slides one finger beneath her curled pinky, presses against her pillowed palm, and recognizes the crumble of dry grit. Extracting his finger, the favorite father sees that it's covered in red. The stove's electric coils blush behind them, and the smallest sister smiles. "Rustblood," the favorite father says.

The Smallest Sister Decides to Make Herself Red

often. She crushes the sun into her collarbone. She strings corroded washers into a necklace. She dresses her lips in the sanguine river water and sucks the stain from pipes behind the aluminum plant, leaving a trail of crust down her throat. Her words emerge already weathered with rust, and she feels herself grow older with each one—older than the oldest sister, older than the quiet mother, older even, she thinks, than the mill the favorite father loves so much. When he touches her, she is as old as the city that folds in like a fist around them.

The Favorite Father Gets Home from Work

and sets his lunch pail on the table. He shakes himself off like a dog, and the smallest sister watches as clumps of gathered rust fall from his chafed arms and legs. Some scatter across the floor. Some form a pile of platelets at his feet. Some disintegrate immediately with all of his mistakes.

The Favorite Father is Sorry

when the smallest sister stretches her body out, the length of a mother. She spills herself onto the kitchen floor before him, feigning pain. She counts out eleven names for him, her favorite, and ties them around herself like a tourniquet—tight—until an August inside her bursts with orange light that surges up to her head and blooms in her mouth, suddenly full of ruffling sounds from eleven newborn leaves, curled inside the calyx of her tongue.

With a pinky, the favorite father unfurls her words. One by one he tastes them, oily on his lips. "Sorry," he says when he is done, and this name is her favorite one.

The Oldest Sister Teaches

the smallest about their city—"our history," she says. They sit in the basin of an empty swimming pool, bottoms sunk into the deep layer of red dust that's collected there. Beside the rusting ladder, now stepless, a child's handprint recedes into the concrete. Rust has gathered in the wells of its fingertips. The smallest sister tries to fit her hand inside of it, but she is already too big. She hugs her knees to her neck then and imagines her body impossibly small. Self-shrunken, she curls inside the womb of her sister's ear and listens:

In the Century of Fumes

the city was full of tin-can men
who cracked their morning
eggs on their foreheads.

Often, a wife watched the yolk
slide down her tinny man's
face into the pan,
where the egg squealed
and blackened.

The men liked the smell of it
burning, and filled themselves
with that smell of smoke
coiled inside
their tin-can rib cages,
pythons inside
those tin-can throats.

In the Century of Mute Tongues

women sucked stingers
from garden bees. They stung
themselves once before bed, twice

in the morning sun. Wordless,
they made enemies

of their venomous men
who took mute tongues
for happy ones.

In the Century of Hot Air

the sky over the city sagged
like a threadbare dress, tired of all
the heat that seeped from the mouths

of its smoke-throated men. Clouds
whimpered to the ground, balloons
let down. Women fanned

smoke from their homes, chased
gray tufts like rodents
onto neighbors' lawns.

The scent of singed grass
was slow to leave the city.

In the Century of Tiny Earthquakes

the city coughed until the smoke had cleared.
      People grew so used to the constant,

subtle quaking that when the city stilled itself,
      they found they had to dance, room to room,

gyrating past one another like spintops. In need
      of music, dancing women began to hum,

but still refused to move their tongues. Their men
      resolved to hold them still until

stone mouths softened with moss or crumbled.

In the Century of New Skin

children split like bad cells

into a frenzy of more children.
The city squirmed with them,

an ant-laden peony, sinking
into its grass, blooming
black from black.

In the Century of Birthmarks

parents held their newborns up
to the sun and read the shadows
cast through them like runes.

They found tableaus in blood—
each life sketched in blue lines
along the arms and thighs.

But if their veins sang of ruin,
babies were marked with anklets
to tell each doom apart:

slowborns from oldborns from
illborns from coldborns from those
whose blood refused the light.

In the Century of Breaking Sentences

words swelled with earnestness and burst
between teeth like overripe grapes.

The verbose were found choked
on their own superfluous vociferousness,
adjectives stuck like seeds to their chins.

Sentences drooped like old vines, half-empty.
Scraps of dropped conversations grew
black and rancid in the streets. Eventually,

the city was strung with dried up phrases,
brittle echoes of even the dead,
whose words still burned for ears.

The Roller Coaster is Burning, the Favorite

father tells his daughters, buttoning their chin and ear flaps.
"We've got to get pictures," he says.

The sky chews its orange lip of horizon and furrows into smoke
as the trio walks in a line of red caps. They are a lit fuse, travelling
into the combusting heart of the city's amusement park.

When they arrive swathed in ash, the roller coaster is folded in half,
a writhing lattice of ruptured tracks, gangly as a giant insect.
Hugging an arched belly of metal cars, its corroded arms are
crossed already—the death pose, the smallest sister knows. She
watches it shrink into a molten fist of steel and splinters, forging
itself to the scrap-laden earth.

Walking home, she imagines the coaster underground, the sound of
thunder rumbling backward beneath her, an ever-nearing earthquake
that never breaks the surface.

The Oldest Sister Follows

the smallest sister after school one day, toeing through gravel-pocked snow. As they pass the gymnasium, their shadows feather and the brick erodes, leaving two silhouettes pressed into the wall.

The snow is keeping secrets, the oldest sister knows. It teases with the crunch of knuckles or the clack of beads rolling beneath her sneakers. *Shush*, she says, eyes fixed on her sister's back, a red leaf blowing into the black amusement park. *Tchk tchk*, the snow scolds.

Ahead, the smallest sister claps the echo from her hands, scrapes clean her too-small boots, and reaches for a door that the oldest sister has never seen before. But as the door opens, the snow piles itself at the oldest sister's feet, and she trips into a mouthful of pearl and bone. When she looks up, the smallest sister is gone, and the door is closed.

The Smallest Sister Finds

an opening in the burnt amusement park—a door beneath the iron letters DOR, belly of ADORE, the name of the abandoned ballroom, a sign left open-ended. At her ankles, smoke still snakes through the snow. She sucks her jujube of fear, tasting the prick in her chest, a bite on the back of the heart, a rap at her shuttered throat's window. The door swells and splinters blister from the wood, offering themselves. The mottled lock sighs and sucks in a swath of air, clearing the fresh ash in its hollow to expose a bright tongue of magenta paint on the metal. The smallest sister taps the clear knob and it seems to click on, light rushing in to fill the glass facets. Like a mouth, her hand takes the knob wholly into itself, closes, and opens. She sees how, like lips, the door and its frame must always part.

The Smallest Sister Plays

a piano in the ballroom. The spaces between keys are full of red crust and the orange-stained ivory is jamming, cracking up. The song is stuck, a tongue in a throat, a bird on a leash, a boomerang. She plays faster, but the keys are fracturing like glass. Limp with splinter-slits, her fingertips can barely tap them.

Determined, she turns over her hand, knuckles down, and drags a bony song out. But the piano now is just a rusty boat full of broken teeth. The song is nothing but a sack full of feathers tied to a string.

The Ballroom

is gutted, a three-walled hollow unfolding around the oldest sister as she enters and listens for echoes. Thick with sistersong, the air inside coruscates with flakes of snow and rust. Whorls of rotting confetti hurl up from the ground with the flutter of a hundred baby tongues. She tries to trap them, casting her arms into the black, stirring herself. But the air puckers where she touches it, tightening around her.

As she leaves, she shuts the ballroom door behind her and hears a double shudder: inside, the stage, on its one good leg, teeters, then slumps into the orchestra pit; outside, blackened song bits lift from the wells of her ears, float up the waxy canals, and waft into the winter around her, coating the snow.

At Home, the Oldest Sister Whistles

the melody she heard the smallest sister playing in the ballroom. The song paints the walls of their house with red, and tiny ears sprout along the floor's edge just to catch the runoff. Tiny ears listen all night under the beds.

In the morning, the quiet mother stumbles over a miniature earlobe, looks down, and bends close to examine its delicate folds. She traces them with her pinky, thinking of a lullaby. But instead of a song, she whispers her name into the ear. She says it over and over, becoming her own echo.

The House Wakes

the next day, but the quiet mother can't get out of bed. Through the window, the sun shifts its blanket of light onto her side, then slowly pulls it back again.

Another night knocks, but still she doesn't stir.

The oldest sister sits beside her mother in the dark, touching her hair, red-dusted and braided with ribbons of gray. She tries to take her mother's face in her hands, but finds already it's filled with lead.

The Oldest Sister Reads

what the red mites write on the sidewalk when she lingers: a silent score she could sing in her sleep—she's read this one before.

She had a favorite too, a name the quiet mother erased as she swept his boot prints from the porch. For years, the floorboards in the oldest sister's bedroom creaked his name beneath her feet, so the quiet mother never entered that room.

Now the oldest sister crushes the mites on the concrete with her fingers, one by one—little bursts of memory undone.

Spring-Cleaning, the Quiet Mother

discovers the habit of touching that's begun in her kitchen. It wafts like a sulfur perfume through all of her rooms. She finds burnt sugar cubes of touching stashed under beds and salt mounds of touching collected on tabletops. She stirs them into pots of boiled apple skins, russet carvings that arrange themselves into scenes.

Turning the kitchen corner one day, she falls into a drift of it: his hand on her smallest daughter like stale sweetbread dipped in syrupy red.

Trying Anger, the Quiet Mother

comes to him with clacking bell tongues, but when she tosses them, they soften—just a scattering of sighs across the floor. The favorite father folds at the waist, groaning. He gathers the orphaned tongues in the tin cup of his hand and rattles them into rain. Rain huddles beneath the awnings, yawning at the window, and the house is consumed by the mundane plash of water shattering itself.

Penance

Woman, lay my hands
in the skillet, he pleads,
sear these palms clean.

Instead, she boils him
down. She skims
the foam and scoops him
up with her fingernails.

She shovels him into her
mouth. She whittles
him down to a bone-
shaped lip of skin,
the softest frown.

Downstairs, the New Neighbors

are having laughs with their new dog. Upstairs in bed, the favorite father can hear the laughs trickling up through cracks in the old floorboards. They are the low laughs of the happily married, each one like a bubble that's swum through warm milk and surfaced in a burst like a clap for the snow-haired dog running laps around the pinewood table. The favorite father knows these are not the sticky tar laughs of conflicted lovers, nor the paperweight laughs of the lonely, which drop in great thuds.

Beside him, the quiet mother pretends to sleep. She knows the walls of the new neighbors' apartment are white as bone, dust-free. Later, when she begins to snore quietly, her low growls ooze down through the cracks in the floorboards and fall unheard past the sleeping dog, landing in great globs at the feet of the new neighbors' pinewood table.

In the morning, the favorite father tries to rouse the quiet mother with a laugh, but it falls out tinny and crumpled. Over and over, he tries, throwing his broken laughs against her reddening cheek, but today she refuses to wake.

Wife Song

Like copper, you bent
and swayed beneath me,

but tarnished with touch—
a curl of verdigris

etched behind each ear,
scars that followed

my vinegar fingers. How deep
the trails of blue and green

I left in your body,
how immediate—love,

what impatient decay.

The Quiet Mother Won't Forgive

herself for this: one hand around a jar of fire ants, one hand spooning them carefully into a yellow lunch box. A few spill from the spoon and hover on the wind of her breath before they fall to the bottom of the box, where they gather themselves into the corners. They look just like bits of rust there, trembling against the yellow. *I can't be blamed*, she thinks, *for what is too delicate.*

At school that day, the smallest sister doesn't look beneath the stacked packages of food when she opens the yellow lunchbox. She listens to the crinkle of plastic wrappers and imagines she is opening a suitcase of nervous leaves. She eats a sugar cake, licks the cold grit around her teeth, and doesn't see the red ants scaling the box's yellow walls, the ants falling in little balls of red onto her lap. She doesn't notice them at all until she stands and feels the ants dribble down her thigh, single-file. They crawl as if threaded, beads on a string, one hundred hot teeth needling her leg.

The Quiet Mother Moves

like breath, in and out of the house. Like a lung, the house empties
and fills.

IV

The Oldest Sister Speaks

to the smallest in a voice like dripping water, meaning pooling around the corners of her mouth, eating through her vowels. A few sounds fall to the ground, but when the smallest sister tries to gather them in her hands, they leak through her fingers. So with one thumb hooked into her sister's cheek, she peers into the dark behind her teeth and finds, etched under her tongue, the story her sister has been trying to tell:

In the Century of Lunch Pails

the city sprouted silver flues
like glistening ears on a wrinkled tuber,

which listened as coverlets of wind, cut
from the sky, dropped through them.

Everywhere the chew of pipes branching
through copper soil could be heard.

Everywhere the groan and whistle of liquid
aluminum, churning the river to a radiant loam.

Everywhere the whisper ticks of fingers,
every hand a clock. And every evening,

the clinking, ever nearer the doorstep, of coins
inside all the hollowed-out fathers as they walked.

In the Century of Silences

production of words was cut
to save money. First adverbs
and adjectives became seasonal,
but never returned. Then transitive
verbs—nothing an object anymore.

Eventually the city was down
to just nouns and connective threads—
a tapestry already half unraveled.

After layoffs, only prepositions
and articles remained, baby aspirins
held tenderly on infant lips.

Expressions of love balanced
awkwardly on the tongue:
the *a* above a *the*, with a *beside*
underneath the *toward*,
an *after* behind the *before.*

When the plant closed, no
exclamations were heard,
but the city opened with the pink
of a thousand gapemouths, all
of its citizens miming themselves.

In the Century of Records

words returned under municipal jurisdiction, and lives
were organized under titles like:
>   *Showers Three Times a Day*
>   *Seven Sweaters*
>   *Loves Salad*
>   *Runs from Bees*
>   *Watches Dogs Bury Bones*
>   *Patient Shaver*
>   *Childhood Burn Scars*
>   *Slow Blinker*
>   *Estranged Son*
>   *Professor of Logic*
>   *Blind from Birth*

Some of these were misfiled serendipitously:
>   *Flowers, Three Times a Day*
>   *Rents for Peas*
>   *Patient-saver*

some tragically:
>   *Severe Sweater*
>   *Less Solid*
>   *Catches Dogs, Buries Bones*
>   *Child that Burns Cars*
>   *Slob, Licker*
>   *Professional Juke*

and others were lost altogether:
>   *Bluffed Her Birth*

In the Century of Research

dirty laundry dredged from the city vault was piled
into lights, darks, and reds—the most difficult to cleanse.

The orchard of family trees, found to be rotten, was chopped up
for rocking chairs, breadboxes, and banana hammocks.

The library of records was opened to the public, and a rush
of great-grandchildren writing memoirs stampeded through

the labyrinth of corridors, which were organized by the third letters
of town surnames—one letter to a book, one book to a room.

Those with ancestral deadbeats, slobberers, and over-perspiring
sneaks opened the mammoth books and gasped all at once,

sending a flood of dust winding through the library
and into the streets, tearing down doors all over the city.

In the Century of Dusty Hallways

children slogged through clusters of it,
scooping up coughs, whooping
family secrets loose. As houses shook

with wheezes, incessant sneezing
dragged on like a clubfoot
one simply learned to work around.

Through kitchen windows
the city funneled, a thousand panes
of glass rattling in their frames.

In the dark, crickets were drowned
out by the creaking of beds beneath
those who sneezed in their sleep.

Often, mothers caught one another
by the river at night, eyes wide,
arms locked to brooms. Often,

they agreed to make another secret
of their sweeping, and no one knew

how much of the city's past
the water had swallowed.

In the Century of Dirty Water

children found three hundred bluegill
dead in the river every morning—

a crowd of bloated bellies turned cloudward.
Invisible cradles rocking, the silent fish

bodies would glint and cut the sun to slivers,
tossing shards of light back into the sky.

Still, the children returned every day
to the banks, searching for hints

of a world behind them. Caught
and thrown by the water, only their own
shattered voices came back.

In the Century of Mandatory Crying

it was decreed that the solution
to dirty water was a salt washout—
a man-made flood. One
half hour daily for the average citizen.

But mothers whose children admitted
to panning the river for secrets
were expected to weep through entire days—

wet spots on the fresh bed sheets,
salt stains on the polished mantle,
little drops on the dinner filets.

In the Century of Waiting

the water finally subsided, leaving
rings of red like incriminating lip prints
on the steel face of the city.

In the Century of Rust

the city's shoulders glittered with fiery dust.
Dramatic, wind-driven, it cloaked every citizen,
and found its way into each
of the body's hollows.

It fell from their mouths in scabs
when they sang too loud, yawned too long
or sighed too heavily. It left

iron orange streaks on their tongues
when they kissed, so it was always apparent
when two had been kissing. They had to

brush their hands nightly along each
other's spines just to keep their backs

from rusting out—*that stuff*,
mothers would say to one another,
will eat through anything.

The Quiet Mother Hides

inside a maze of numbered streets lined with bungalows. Behind the First Street is the Second Street, and inside the Second Street is the Third Street, and at the center of the Third Street lies the Fourth Street—paved in a circle so that the houses there can stare at each other all night and never feel lonely. Each bungalow is made of four tin sheets, two windows, and no door. The sun slinks around the bungalows restlessly—a light that looks from tin sheet to tin sheet, then falls blinking into the street, dizzy as a holiday.

Some evenings, the smallest sister comes to the Fourth Street to sit outside her mother's new home. Feet tucked beneath her in the road, she watches the quiet mother through the bungalow's front window. Usually the quiet mother is combing rust from her hair just as the sun slides into the bungalow through the opposite window and sets itself behind her. Etched by its light, she becomes an antique in the smallest sister's eyes—oxidized at the knees and elbows, her feet already settling into a fine patina.

Wife Song

You were brass when I left,
throwing my hands up, finally,

to your chest—a gong
that rang sweet and deep,

unyielding. You left
my knuckles bruised

and pulpy as rotten grapes,
blister wrung and stinging—

in my ears, lunatic
aftermath of ringing.

The Smallest Sister Presses Coal to Her Palm

in the junkyard. Sitting next to a bag of black charcoal, she pets the
briquette as one pets a turtle's shell—with two ginger fingers and a
longing to see it react. It doesn't. A nearby tire shivers, or just the
wind inside it—the smallest sister doesn't know. She takes the
briquette and slides it along the tallow white of her thigh, scrubbing
its black into her skin. Empty of wind, the nearby tire watches as she
rubs herself sooty and red, rubs until there is nothing left.

The Oldest Sister is an Indian Giver

who takes her word back. The word is *killdeer* and it swoops from her mouth when she lets it out for the first time. The smallest sister watches it slice the wind in loops of flight as scallops of air fall like crepe paper around her shoes.

It is months later when the oldest sister brings a robin home, its head the color of a bruise. The smallest sister watches its chest fill and shrivel, an orange balloon in the oldest sister's hand. Rust is wedged like scales into the crevices between its feathers. It lifts one wing, heavy with corrosion. Beneath the downy underwing, strings of brown stretch and drip like maple syrup. The smallest sister wants to taste it. Suddenly the robin throws its left wing into circles, slicing the air, and the smallest sister shouts, "Killdeer!" But at the word, the bird stops moving, and the oldest sister says never to say it again.

The Favorite Father Chases a Tornado

through the river with his camera. A layer of rust floating like algae on the water begins to break up. As he wades, his legs part one red island, making another. Soon there are too many tiny rust islands to count, and the river is a mottled red-brown.

His daughters watch from the banks. The smallest pulls up tufts of grass, and the oldest pats them back into the ground. Uprooted bits of steel fly from the soil and land like shrapnel around them. The oldest sister lays the loose grass blades across her sister's knee and chucks the metal into the water.

"You broke it," the smallest sister says to the favorite father, but he doesn't hear. He's getting his shot. "The river is ruined," she says.

The oldest sister shakes her head. The sky troubles itself and fills with orange funnels, but none can touch the earth.

The Smallest Sister Coughs

up her house in pieces, hand over her lips, smothering the
clang of wood and steel against her molars. She looks
around the playground, then looks down. In her fist, a pool
of spit and flotsam: orange peels of rust, soot blossoms, grains
of plaster. A curl of twine dangles from her mouth. She pulls it out
and binds the pile into a chewed up pit. With one thumb she pushes
it down into the brassy soil, where ruin swells and blooms, tumors
of memory underground.

The Favorite Father Pours

himself into the river, his past a platinum stream that dims with a
broken hiss as it hits the water, the sound from his mouth like a
name snuffed out.

The Oldest Sister Braids

her fingers into a tangled curse, a secret woven between them like garish copper peeking through a rubber-wrapped electrical cord. She hides bright sheaves of rust in a faded photo book, corroding the mouths and noses pressed against the red. Each page folds over with the groan of an iron gate, an invitation. The trap door in her ear opens and a troupe of chickadees waltzes into her head's tin ballroom on their needle feet, accusing: *tock tick tick.* But the oldest sister calls them down. She drowns them in the basement of herself, then dredges them up again, each feather a sodden smirk, each body a limp apology.

The Smallest Sister Sleeps

outside, pulled into a fold of pavement. Pebbles press their hundred fingers against her back. In the morning, she filches sun-hot pennies from the street. She tests the tacky tops with her teeth and stacks them in her mouth like wafers, copper penance cakes. The gummy face of Lincoln greens under her tongue, and the flashy taste of shame bounces around like light from a mirror shifting inside her.

The Quiet Mother Knocks

on her tin wall, but her knuckles suck the sound up immediately,
leaving only the tick of bones chattering inside her fingers like
babies' teeth.

At the Edge of the City

wastewater tanks squat like the sorry fists of old men, time-peeled. Water seeps from them as from clenched knuckles—an inevitable dribble—and the ground dazzles with it: amber, chartreuse, aubergine, puce. The smallest sister weaves between the fists, wind-kicked, a black leaf. She spots something in a tank a few yards away: a trash bag drifting in lazy circles. It looks to her like a girl, skimming: she sees a black-coated back travelling the circumference of the tank, cutting liquid seams, and she watches the water stitch itself together in the girl's wake. How tiring, the smallest sister thinks—the work of separation never complete.

The City Opens

along its river-seam like a swollen belly, expelling antiques. The smallest sister makes a list of what she finds on the banks. Parts for prying: fire poker, pen knife, battle axe, beer cans, crowbar. Parts for moving forward: copper piping, clock gears, bicycle spokes. Parts for staying put: slating nails, vice grip, hammers—ball peen, claw head, dead blow. Parts for lifting heavy things: steel tongs, crane arms, spring coils, fender wings. Every night she finds more, so she begins to build herself a home from them. Every night another wall, every week another room, every month another house—her new city birthed from the refuse.

The Smallest Sister is Radiant

inside. Patient under her tongue, a word waits like a grenade of rust, fool's gold, and what else she can't say.

She can't say why she swallows the word, but when she does she knows it will burst in her throat one day.

She knows the scraps will scatter like buckshot and burrow downward, lodging in all of her hollows. Industrious shovels, the shreds of rust and rock let loose will cultivate a network of tunnels for light to seep through.

Gold flakes will settle into the spaces between her vertebrae, crumbling over time into a fine dust that will coat the lobes of her lungs with glittering stillness.

She can't say when it will arrive, but she knows at the moment of death, she will be brilliant. Her body will shine like a city inside.

Rochelle Hurt was born and raised in the Ohio Rust Belt. She holds an MFA from the University of North Carolina in Wilmington, and she has been awarded prizes from *Crab Orchard Review*, *Arts & Letters*, *Hunger Mountain*, and *Poetry International*. Rochelle's poetry and prose have also appeared in various literary journals, including *The Kenyon Review*, *The Southeast Review*, *The Cincinnati Review*, and *Mid-American Review*. Currently, she lives in Cincinnati, Ohio, with her cat, Frida.

Author photo: Doug Diesenhaus

THE MARIE ALEXANDER POETRY SERIES

Founded in 1996 by Robert Alexander, the Marie Alexander Poetry Series is dedicated to promoting the appreciation, enjoyment, and understanding of American prose poetry. Currently an imprint of White Pine Press, the series publishes one to two books annually. These are typically single-author collections of short prose pieces, sometimes interwoven with lineated sections, and an occasional anthology demonstrating the historical or international context within which American poetry exists. It is our mission to publish the very best contemporary prose poetry and to carry the rich tradition of this hybrid form on into the 21st century.

Series Editor: Robert Alexander
Editor: Nickole Brown

Volume 18
The Rusted City
Rochelle Hurt

Volume 17
Postage Due
Julie Marie Wade

Volume 16
Family Portrait: American Prose Poetry 1900–1950
Edited by Robert Alexander

Volume 15
All of Us
Elisabeth Frost

Volume 14
Angles of Approach
Holly Iglesias

Volume 13
Pretty
Kim Chinquee

Volume 12
Reaching Out to the World
Robert Bly

Volume 11
The House of Your Dream: An International Collection of Prose Poetry
Edited by Robert Alexander and Dennis Maloney

Volume 10
Magdalena
Maureen Gibbon

Volume 9
The Angel of Duluth
Madelon Sprengnether

Volume 8
Light from an Eclipse
Nancy Lagomarsino